Authentic

FAITH

Authentic FAITH

101 Keys to Experiencing Real Relationship with God

David McLaughlan

BARBOUR
PUBLISHING

© 2013 by Barbour Publishing, Inc.

Print ISBN 978-1-62416-627-3

eBook Editions:
Adobe Digital Edition (.epub) 978-1-62836-247-3
Kindle and MobiPocket Edition (.prc) 978-1-62836-248-0

Published by Barbour Publishing, Inc., P.O. Box 719, Uhrichsville, Ohio 44683, www.barbourbooks.com

Our mission is to publish and distribute inspirational products offering exceptional value and biblical encouragement to the masses.

 Member of the
Evangelical Christian
Publishers Association

Printed in the United States of America.

Contents

Section 2: At Church

Section 6: In Prayer

Section 1

_____

IN YOUR PERSONAL WALK

1. Be of Service

Jesus was served on occasion. He was angry on occasion. He was sad, felt pain, and died and rose again. But mostly Jesus served.

Jesus baptized others. He comforted John in jail, fed the hungry, talked to the outcast, and healed and healed and healed. . . . He was all about relieving the suffering of others and loving the unloved.

Jesus' earthly ministry could be summed up as praising the Father and serving others. He probably didn't see much of a distinction between the two things.

So, if ever you find yourself in a situation where you are asking, "What would Jesus do?" the answer will probably be "Serve!"

> *The greatest among you must be a servant.*
> MATTHEW 23:11 NLT

- Don't ask, "Are you all right?" Ask, "What can I do for you?" instead.

- The Good Samaritan was the person others least expected to see serving. If he could do it, you can, too.

2. Be Still

"Be still and know that I am God." It's what they call counterintuitive. In other words it doesn't sound as if it should work. When else can you be still and meet people? Most likely, if you sat still on a sidewalk or in a supermarket, people would deliberately avoid you!

We move and we do stuff to meet people—in this world.

Of course, God is in this world and in those people, but those encounters come with a lot of distractions. (It might be raining, or you might not be able to believe she wore those shoes with that top!)

But God is also beyond the world. So, if you just want to meet Him, find a quiet place, close your eyes, let all thoughts of the world leave your mind. Whatever else there is—will be God!

> *Be still, and know that I am God: I will be exalted among the heathen, I will be exalted in the earth.*
> PSALM 46:10 KJV

- It should take no effort to be still, but it's surprisingly difficult. Take time to find the perfect "still place."

- God is already there. Be patient with yourself until you learn to see Him.

3. Find God in Others

God breathed life into Adam. It's hard to imagine God needing air, like us. But whatever He breathed into the first man, it was life and it was of Himself. He is where life came from, and, as descendants of the first humans, we all carry something of God within us.

That alone would be worthy of respect, no matter how the particular recipient had treated their gift.

The other end of the story is where that "God stuff," will be set free from flesh and blood in heaven.

In between the beginning and that never-ending end, however, some people make it very difficult indeed to see anything of God in them. That's because they themselves don't believe it. They have been tricked into thinking that they are less than creations of Love.

That's when the work needs to be done. That's when we have to remind them of just how wonderful they are. But first of all we have to see it in them and believe it ourselves.

And the LORD God formed man of the dust of the ground,
and breathed into his nostrils the breath of life;
and man became a living soul.
GENESIS 2:7 KJV

- Imagine the person as a baby, fresh from God. Wonder what happened.

- Children carry family traits. If the resemblance to their heavenly Father isn't obvious (and it usually isn't), don't be put off.

4. Give Up

Would you define yourself by the gifts you received for your birthday? It might be nice to be known as the lady with the ridiculously expensive shoes or the guy with the portrait his three-year-old painted of him. But those things wouldn't really define you.

Some people do associate themselves very much with their status, their houses, the cars they drive. Those things, no less than birthday presents, are gifts. Okay, you have to work for them, but the ability to work is, in itself, a gift.

None of these objects define you in God's eyes. He loves you for what you are behind all that stuff. He would love you just the same if it all disappeared tomorrow.

Giving things up—be it for Lent, or to help someone else, or just to see if you can—is a reminder that you are not defined by the things you surround yourself with. You are defined by God's love!

Then he said to them, "Watch out!
Be on your guard against all kinds of greed;
life does not consist in an abundance of possessions."
LUKE 12:15 NIV

- Ask yourself what you couldn't live without. Try it. Fill the space with an offering to God.

- Ask yourself if there is anything you do that you wouldn't care to explain to God. Get rid of it.

5. Read Messages from Bygone Times

It makes sense that those who lived closer to Jesus' time would have a better understanding of Him. But nothing about Jesus makes earthly sense. Two thousand years later, you and I can know Him as well as those who walked the earth immediately after Him.

You might think that books written in the first, second, and third centuries AD would be old-fashioned. But Jesus taught about things that never go out of fashion. Those old texts are still worth reading. They became old texts because they spoke to so many people in the ages between then and now, people in different times and different situations.

So take advantage of the lessons they learned! You will find that, once you get past the old-fashioned language, they are still as relevant as ever.

A wise man will hear, and will increase learning;
and a man of understanding shall attain unto wise counsels.
PROVERBS 1:5 KJV

- Remember, a thing isn't valuable just because it's old. Use discernment.

- Many books and texts on faith are more available than ever before, thanks to the Internet. Take pastoral advice about which would be useful.

6. Travel the Road to Emmaus

The travelers on the road to Emmaus knew about Jesus' death and had heard of His resurrection. They didn't know what to believe. The Lord put them right in a few words.

The point is that they traveled quite a distance with Him before understanding who He was.

We will travel with many people throughout our lives. Some will be in for the long haul; others might walk beside us for a few minutes. God will have put them there for a purpose. It might be that we should help them, or they might help us. We might teach them something, or they might teach us.

But, if nothing at all comes from the encounter, then something has probably been missed somewhere.

Let's try and make sure that happens as little as possible, making each journey our own version of the road to Emmaus, knowing that Jesus will be walking with us somewhere.

As they talked and discussed these things, Jesus himself
suddenly came and began walking with them.
But God kept them from recognizing him.
LUKE 24:15–16 NLT

- Take time for people. Imagine finding you had rushed past Jesus.

- See the coffee you give, the directions you supply, or the friendly word as offerings to God.

7. Remember Heroes of the Faith

Heroes of the faith generally have this in common—they were ordinary people lifted to extraordinary heights by their belief in the Lord. Because it's not the kind of "career" where wealth or connections are any advantage, they were mostly people ordinary folk can relate to.

We know that what happened to them could also happen to us. What a great encouragement!

Reading about such heroes helps expand our awareness of the wonderful path we are walking along. Reading those same tales to our children might have a longer-lasting effect than all the secular adventure stories in the world put together.

When we remind ourselves of what people like us went through for their faith and what the outcomes were, it can't help but put our own trials into perspective and boost our expectations of a wonderful outcome!

Paul lived and worked with them,
for they were tentmakers just as he was.
ACTS 18:3 NLT

- Start a "heroes" library and share with friends.

- Look out for the heroes of faith around you who might never have movies made of their lives.

8. Care for Yourself

The expression used to be "treat your body like a temple," but, given what went on in some temples, it wasn't very helpful.

Try to remember the most expensive gift your parents ever gave you, whether it was a musical instrument, a car, or whatever. What was the last thing they said before you took it away? "Take care of it!"

They had invested a lot in getting it for you; they wanted it to last, to be treated with respect.

The body you walk around in is one of the most complex things ever. It has more potential than just about anything.

I listened to a man who had provided his son with a job, a place of his own, money, all to bring him back from the wrong side of the law. The heartbreak was obvious as he told how his son consistently chose a self-destructive life.

God must feel the same when we treat the beautiful bodies He gave us so casually.

Perhaps you were too young to "take care of it" when you got that expensive birthday gift. Maybe now you understand where your parents were coming from, and maybe you'll frustrate God a little less than you did them.

Thank you for making me so wonderfully complex!
Your workmanship is marvelous—how well I know it.
PSALM 139:14 NLT

- Man-made or God-grown? The best question to ask about your food.

- Too busy to exercise? Combine it with helping someone. Don't let carelessness limit the life God planned for you.

9. Be Altruistic

Have you ever given away cash you needed to someone who needs it more? Have you ever skipped dinner so your children might be better fed? Have you ever gone on a missions trip or simply taken time out a busy schedule to help someone?

That's altruism, and it might be the one thing those who believe in a God-free universe can never explain. The noncreationist view has life coming about by accident and then striving to survive simply for the sake of it.

Altruism has no place in that worldview. Helping others survive sometimes lessens our chances of thriving. There is no rational explanation for that—if we were *not* creatures of a giving, sacrificing God!

When we give when we are not obliged to, when we would be better off not giving, we follow our Father's example, and He will surely be smiling.

For all these have of their abundance cast in unto
the offerings of God: but she of her penury hath
cast in all the living that she had.
LUKE 21:4 KJV

- Help someone who can't help you back—
  and help them generously.

- Don't be surprised when God rewards you.
  He doesn't want anyone to suffer for helping
  his children.

10. Learn from Elders

An old folk saying tells us "the evening knows what the morning doesn't even suspect."

When I was searching for faith, I needed to have a whole bunch of questions answered, several sheets of lists with boxes checked off. Once I got here, I found a level of knowledge I hadn't even suspected, knowledge that left my previous questions completely redundant.

When we are teenagers, we can't imagine our parents could ever teach us anything. Then, when we get to be parents ourselves, we wish we had listened.

So as confident, as educated, as worldly-wise as we might think we are now, let us never imagine we can't learn a lot from people who have walked with God longer than us.

Just remember, the evening knows things the morning, the lunchtime, the afternoon, and the rush hour never even suspect.

Is not wisdom found among the aged?
Does not long life bring understanding?
JOB 12:12 NIV

- People who have acquired the wealth of a lifetime often just want someone to listen. Be that one.

- Don't dismiss what you don't understand. It may not be the time to understand, but still remember.

11. Learn from Children

We learn a lot of things in our lives—the names of the colors, the alphabet, math, spelling, the rules of the games we play at recess, cooking, driving, how to play an instrument, how far we drive a sit-on mower up a slope, what it feels like to have our hearts broken, how not to break someone's heart, how to study for qualifications, how to translate those qualifications into a salary, how to climb the promotion ladder, how to disinfect soccer wounds, how to manage our finances, how to lose someone we love, how tightly a tiny hand can grip our fingers, and so on and so on.

Some of these things are important when it comes to living an earthly life. But many of them are completely irrelevant to our heavenward journey. The things you really need for that you will have learned while still a child. When children trust, they trust completely; when they love, they love unconditionally.

Whatever else we fill our heads with in this life, we need to not let them crowd out the really important stuff—the things we learned as children.

Verily I say unto you, Except ye be converted, and become as little children, ye shall not enter into the kingdom of heaven.
MATTHEW 18:3 KJV

- Tell Bible stories to little ones. Talking in terms they understand will simplify the lessons—for them and for you.

- Ask the children what they think of the stories. Take on board what they say.

12. Practice Trust

Have you ever attended one of those workplace team-building sessions? The most popular exercises involve building trust, like when you close your eyes and topple backward, trusting that one of your colleagues will catch you before you hit the floor!

It's a surprisingly difficult thing to do, but the benefits—as the trainers know—are immense.

If you would like to strengthen your relationship with God, try trusting Him. Testing Him with little things doesn't show much faith—but sometimes we need to ease ourselves in gently.

The more He catches us, the more we become used to His arms around us and the more we want to trust for that same reason.

He might surprise us with the ways He catches us, but, if we trust, He will never let us fall.

So do not throw away this confident trust in the Lord.
Remember the great reward it brings you!
HEBREWS 10.35 NLT

- If there is something the world expects of you, but it wouldn't raise a smile in heaven, try going God's way for a change and see how it works out.

- Stop worrying. Show the world your trust through calm, confident patience.

13. Be Humble

"I wonder what she thinks of me."

So many of our hurts and fears come from trying to live up to what we think other people expect us to be. Sometimes they aren't actually thinking anything about us, so trying to live up to those imagined expectations is doubly sad. We burden ourselves with unnecessary expectations because we think we ought to be better than we are.

Humility sets us free from all that.

Being truly humble means seeing yourself as nothing more than a part of God's creation. But God's creation is wonderful in every aspect, so even the least of His creation is awesome.

Humility sets you free from worrying about what others think of you, and once you don't have that distraction you can truly focus on what God thinks of you.

In my humble opinion, He thinks you are great!

True humility and fear of the LORD lead to riches, honor, and long life.
PROVERBS 22:4 NLT

- Put others first in everything. It won't take long to discover how right that feels.

- If someone takes advantage of your humility, don't react negatively, just pray that they one day discover what you know.

14. Give Thanks

Where do I start with this one?

There is the fact that the world is just the right distance from the sun for life to thrive. The fact that it doesn't spin in a perfect circle, so we have seasons. There's that big night-light generously provided for when it's dark. The insects that pollinate our plants. The amazing coincidence that some plants coat their seeds in stuff that's delicious and nutritious for us humans—fruit. There are children—and parents. Not forgetting grandparents! There is the next breath I take, and the one after that. There is chocolate and coffee! Hugs and handshakes. Love!

There's the fact that God never gave up on us "stiff-necked" people, although we tried His patience sorely.

And the more you are grateful for, the more you see to be grateful for! Grateful people are just more fun to be around. They seem to understand God's gift more completely than some others. And I am grateful for them, too!

Give thanks to the LORD and proclaim his greatness.
Let the whole world know what he has done.
1 CHRONICLES 16:8 NLT

- Find a little thing, like the smile of a child or getting to your destination safely, and speak a few words of thanks out loud.

- Thank people, even if they only did their job. You will enjoy it and you might just make their day.

15. Be Hopeful/Avoid Cynicism

The Bible tells us lots of important things. Among them are the facts that God loves us and that His side wins in the end! So, what is there to worry about?

But we still worry.

Despite the assurance that all will be well in the end and that we will be gathered to a wonderful, eternal home, we still fret about bills and the price of gas.

I'm not saying we should ignore these things. We just need to make sure they don't bring us down, weaken our faith—or make us a bad advertisement for it.

Whenever you feel worried or cynical, take a metaphorical step back. Take the long view. Realize that these little trials aren't sent by God to teach us patience; they are sent by His enemy as a distraction.

Smile and step away. Swap cynicism for certainty. Remember that these little annoyances will be the first things you forget in heaven.

Why, my soul, are you downcast? Why so disturbed within me? Put your hope in God, for I will yet praise him, my Savior and my God.
PSALM 42:5 NIV

- In some company it is fashionable to be cynical. Don't join in. Find something positive to say instead.

- Imagine how excited and positive you feel before going on an exotic vacation. Heaven will be incomparably better!

16. Engage in Missions

Going on a missions trip is often a wonderful experience. Those undertaking the trip will be out of their comfort zone and forced to rely on the Word that brought them there. The people on the receiving end might never have heard the Gospel before and will be enthused by the passion of someone who traveled so far to share it with them.

If you can do such a thing, you definitely should.

But if you can't. . .you can still find a mission in your own town or neighborhood. It will be nonetheless valued by God.

After all, the original missionaries were the apostles. Thomas is believed to have traveled to Africa and India. Philip went to Samaria. Andrew may have traveled to Russia. But, when Paul arrived in Jerusalem, he found some of the apostles were still preaching there.

The best solution may be to make your life a mission, rather than take any one particular trip, and preach the Good News wherever you are.

He said to them, "Go into all the world
and preach the gospel to all creation."
MARK 16:15 NIV

- Find some like-minded friends—and go!

- Ask God where you might be of most use to Him.

17. Engage in Healing

Healing, as in the laying on of hands, is a wonderful thing—but not everyone can make the lame walk or the blind see. In fact, no one can without the Lord!

But no less wonderful is the kind of healing we can all do: the healing of emotional hurts, the bridging of gaps in relationships.

It becomes more difficult when it comes to addressing the wounds in our own relationships. Because, after all, we have good reasons for not talking to. . .whomever.

But those reasons never wash with God. He just wants the wounds healed, and it's down to you to swallow your pride and do whatever it takes to get it done.

You think that's hard? Try healing the rift between other people and God. If you can convince someone who's hurt or fear has left them wanting nothing to do with faith to come wholeheartedly to the Lord, that will be a healing that might leave even God feeling better.

He did not say this on his own, but as high priest that year he prophesied that Jesus would die for the Jewish nation, and not only for that nation but also for the scattered children of God, to bring them together and make them one.
JOHN 11:51–52 NIV

- Put aside pride and every "good" reason (except your safety.) Reach out to someone you would rather not talk to. Tell yourself you are doing it for God, if it helps.

- Remember, God isn't waiting for someone else to heal the wound. He wants you to do it!

18. Watch for "Serendipity"

According to the legend of Serendip, three princes are sent on a journey by their father in order to gain wisdom. On the way to the land of Serendip various chance occurrences give them the wisdom they need to rule their father's kingdom.

Doesn't it seem as if "chance" might have been on their side?

In a world created by and permeated by God, there is no such thing as chance. Like the princes, you and I are on a journey. Like them, we are here to learn so we, too, might wear crowns in our Father's kingdom.

We might not have the wisdom to understand all the things that happen by "chance" around us, but if we keep asking, "Father, what are you telling me here?" it will come.

If we are here for any purpose, it is to prepare for the kingdom to come. Keep learning along the way!

Then I saw, and considered it well:
I looked upon it, and received instruction.
PROVERBS 24:32 KJV

- Take the time to think about new or unusual occurrences. Don't rush on by without at least trying to understand something of them.

- Talk to friends in faith. Share your insights and ask for their thoughts.

19. Appreciate True Science

We tend to think of science and faith as being opposites, but it hasn't always been that way.

The first scientists were men of faith. Everyone else was busy farming or fighting. Monks alone had the time to ponder how the universe worked. The separation came later, and even now many scientists have a deep faith. They understand that science tells us how—but never why!

Take that simple substance, water. Science tells us it is made of hydrogen and oxygen. Hydrogen is explosive, and oxygen enables things to burn. The two mixed together should be highly combustible. Instead, water puts fires out. How does that work? Magic? Or something more powerful? Something more real?

Don't fall into the trap of thinking it's a competition with science on one side and faith on the other. The more science discovers, the more wonderful God seems!

Do you know how the clouds are set in heaven, the great works of Him Who is perfect in understanding?
JOB 37:16 NLV

- Don't indulge in a "them and us" attitude to science and its adherents. Look instead for the wonders and delight in them.

- Remember, science tells how, faith tells why. Ideally, we want to know both (even if the why is more important!)

20. Find a Sacred Space

Do you and your spouse have a special place? It might be where you went on that first date. It might be where the big proposal was made. Or it may be a place where you both feel peaceful and comfortable.

Finding a special place for you and God is a bit more difficult. After all, if He is everywhere, how can one place be more significant than any other? We can't give God anything but praise and love—but we can give Him back a little of His own.

Imagine you gave your child a regular allowance. Then one day she came to you with money she had been putting aside. Now she wanted you to spend it on something special for yourself! It would be a completely unnecessary offer—but an incredibly touching gesture nonetheless!

Lay aside a little piece of the world, whether it be a quiet stream, a place in church, or where you kneel at the foot of your bed, just for the Lord. If He loved any part of this world more than all the rest, you can be sure it would be the part a loving child offered back to Him.

*Then Abram removed his tent, and came and
dwelt in the plain of Mamre, which is in Hebron,
and built there an altar unto the LORD.*
GENESIS 13:18 KJV

- Abraham seems to have built altars wherever he
  went. So you could have one at work, one at
  home, one along your favorite walk. . . .

- A personal altar needn't be anything much to
  look at. Just choose a place and say, "I'll meet
  you here, Lord. If that's okay with You."

21. Accept Times of Admonishment

"Don't you ever learn?"

If you are, or have been, a parent of teenagers you will probably have asked that question more than once. It's frustrating, isn't it, when teens can obviously see the best way to go (you are sure), but they still keep making the wrong decisions.

So you might ground them, take away some privileges; you might be tempted to lock them in their rooms. All for their own good!

Of course, they often don't know any better. Physically they might appear mature, but emotionally they might still be children. And they just don't get it!

So, the question is—when did you stop being a child? Of God.

If you find doors closing, if your plans aren't working out, if you start losing privileges, perhaps you ought to stop and try to do what teenagers never seem to do—listen. Accept that Someone with a longer view and a greater understanding thinks you might be going the wrong way. Then try to find the right way.

You will know it by the opening of doors, by the restoration of privileges. . .by your ungrounding.

It is good for me that I have been afflicted;
that I might learn thy statutes.
PSALM 119:71 KJV

- If things aren't going to plan, it's wise to remember—it isn't your plan!

- See times of admonishment not as punishment, but as the further, wonderful, working out of His wisdom. See them as a word to the wise.

22. Beware Times of Plenty

Times of plenty aren't always good times. If two neighbors have next to nothing, they will usually lean on each other, sharing what they have. Doors won't be locked; hard times will be shared, as will successes, because they will usually be earned together.

It might seem to us that more comfort, more material possessions, are things to be desired, but God knows the "poor neighbor" scenario is the better one, because times of plenty often lead to possessiveness, envy, and separation. The possessions will come between you and your neighbor, unless you are aware of that possibility and take steps to make sure it doesn't happen.

How do you do that? By valuing the intangible things like friendship and trust above anything money can buy, by remembering that none of your possessions actually belong to you. God made them, and God will dispose of them in His own time.

Generosity, a good name, humility—those are things you can "own" in bad times and in good.

I know what it is to be in need, and I know what it is to have plenty. I have learned the secret of being content in any and every situation, whether well fed or hungry, whether living in plenty or in want.

PHILIPPIANS 4:12 NIV

- If you find yourself treating people differently in times of plenty, be aware that you are under attack.

- Thank God for all blessings. Affirm to yourself that He can give them or take them and the love will remain the same.

23. Use Love as a Tool

Does that sound cynical to you? Do you think love should be a spontaneous emotional reaction? Sure, it's great when it happens like that.

But an artist can't paint without her brushes. A sculptor can't sculpt without his chisel. A cook needs bowls and rolling pins, and. . .you know.

They are doing a job, they are creating stuff. We are called to help build up a kingdom of God (before the big one comes along.) The best tool for that is love!

You might use it clumsily at first, but you will get better with practice. You'll learn where it's needed and where it's not. (It's needed everywhere, but some places more urgently than others.)

You'll find that love is a tool that does most of the work for you.

Pretty soon you'll be looking at some deliberately created masterpieces! But you don't sign your name on the bottom. You give credit where it's due.

For God is not unrighteous to forget your work and labour of love, which ye have shewed toward his name, in that ye have ministered to the saints, and do minister.
HEBREWS 6:10 KJV

- Be a builder of bridges.

- Actively decide to love the people on both sides of the separation, regardless of your personal feelings. It makes bridge building so much easier.

24. Give. . .

You know the expression, "Give till it hurts"? Well, it only hurts if you don't really want to give.

Once you accept that the money or things you give aren't yours, and it will be replaced, possibly with interest, then giving becomes a real treat.

But don't give as if you are giving. Give as if you are putting the gift back where it belongs, as if it belongs to the other person every bit as much as it belongs to you. Because it's all God's stuff and you are just redistributing it where He wants it put.

So, if it's all God's stuff, what's your input? Well, it's more important than stuff. You get to give the eye contact, the squeeze of a hand, the validation of the other person as a child of God, no more and no less than you.

You might, in practical terms, be increasing their wealth, but in spiritual terms you get to give them the knowledge that they are worth more than any amount of stuff.

But now as for what is inside you—be generous to the poor, and everything will be clean for you.
LUKE 11:41 NIV

- Don't practice giving—practice how you give!

- Don't give to receive. But you will receive. Don't be surprised when it happens. Be loved.

25 . . . And Receive

Most folk think giving is the tricky part, but being able to receive is a skill in itself.

Some of us would give all day every day, if we could, but insist we are fine if someone offers to help us. Or maybe we would accept help—but not ask for it!

Well, here's the thing. You know that good feeling you get when you help; that glow you get from having served the Lord in some little way?

It's not just for you.

The next time someone offers to help you, accept. The next time you need something and no one knows to offer, ask.

If it helps, tell yourself you're not really taking anything from them. You are giving them the gift of that great feeling you love so much, giving them their chance to do good for God. So, really, how generous are you?

The LORD preserveth the simple:
I was brought low, and he helped me.
PSALM 116:6 KJV

- God often provides His help in the form of other people. Don't let pride come between you and the Lord's intention.

- You may be the first one to ask that other guy for help. Imagine how that seed might grow!

26. Affirm the Ones You Love

Who are the ones you love? Who are the ones you are supposed to love?

The answer to the second question is everyone! We are encouraged, nay, commanded, to love one another and to love our enemies. Who does that leave? No one.

It's a great ambition. In reality there will probably be a small, changing, group of loved ones who make this lifelong journey with you. Some will be older, some will be younger, and some will seem more capable than others. But every one of them will struggle at times, and, ideally, every one of them will, at some time or another, help you when you struggle.

One thing alone will see that group safely to the end of their journeys, and that is love. So take it when you need it and give it when you have it.

I long to see you so that I may impart to you some spiritual gift to make you strong—that is, that you and I may be mutually encouraged by each other's faith.
ROMANS 1:11–12 NIV

- Never take it for granted that your family and friends know how you feel about them. Tell them.

- You might never know when someone really needs that word of encouragement, so share it as often as you can.

27. Affirm the Ones You Don't Love

How would it sound if I told you that inside that guy who doesn't give a hoot and inside that gal who prefers the sleazy side of life there was a child of God wanting to get out?

Without getting into the whole nature/nurture debate I can unequivocally state that they were babies once and as close to pure souls as we ever get. After that. . . stuff happened.

Hurts were inflicted, hopes dashed, securities stripped, and bad decisions were made.

Callous/careless/arrogant/violent skins were grown. But the soul, that gift from God, is still in there. It can be encouraged to come out. You might not see the results of your affirmation, but your words might be one more contributor to its eventual freedom.

All you have to do is learn to ignore the ugly and speak love—in the certain belief that the beautiful is in there, listening.

The same came for a witness, to bear witness of the Light,
that all men through him might believe.
JOHN 1:7 KJV

- Brothers and sisters, biological and spiritual, can be hard work, but everyone wants their family to be united.

- The Jew by the roadside and the Good Samaritan might not have talked in any other circumstance. The Samaritan didn't let that stop him. Don't let it stop you.

28. Remember Grace

No I don't mean the old aunt you haven't seen since you were eight. I mean the fact that you are saved by grace. There is nothing more guaranteed to stop us getting too full of ourselves.

No matter how much or how little we have achieved in our lives, the only achievement that matters in the end is accepting Jesus Christ. Only it's not an achievement—it's a gift. The barista who serves the coffee might have received that gift, while the high-flyer he serves it to might not. And vice versa.

So we never ought to feel better—or worse—than anyone else, because one day soon we will meet on a level playing field. If you don't want to be too surprised by whom you meet there (and you don't want them to be surprised to see you), then start treating everyone as if they were recipients of the same gift. Because, even if they haven't received that gift now, they might later.

For the grace of God that bringeth
salvation hath appeared to all men.
TITUS 2:11 KJV

- The expression "there but for the grace of God go I" isn't a self-congratulatory one or a pitying one. It's a reminder that we need to share our gift with the other guy.

- Don't decide in advance who's going to heaven and who's going to hell. Treat everyone you meet as if they are bound for glory. And you might help make that come true.

29. Witness

It's one of the ultimate tests of your faith.

So how do you do it? It easy to say, "I witness through my life. People can see I'm a Christian." But most often all people see is "good folk." You need to say the Name; you need to spread His power.

Sure, it's embarrassing at first! But you never know the good you might do. An ex-addict found love with a Christian girl who heard his testimony. Before that he had only known her as the pharmacy assistant who gave him his medication.

Another man, giving his testimony in public, was shouted down by people from his past—but his estranged son saw something new in him and wanted it.

Testimony is like a charitable offering. You put it out there never knowing the good it might do. The difference is, there is power in the Name, and, when you proclaim it aloud, wonders will occur!

The apostles testified powerfully to the resurrection of the Lord Jesus, and God's great blessing was upon them all.
ACTS 4:33 NLT

- Break yourself in gently. Go along and support a public meeting. Simply be seen with a group of believers.

- A testimony can be given in little ways, at work, with family, but don't leave it to others to guess what you mean. Use the words. Actually talk of your Lord.

30. Talk about Death

I didn't want my daughter to be scared of death. So, when she first raised it in a conversation (at the age of four) I talked about it quite happily. Not being in faith at the time, I outlined all the options as I saw them; just nothing, reincarnation, heaven. . . . The option that most appealed to her was being a ghost. She thought that would be a lot of fun!

As people of faith, we owe it to our families to take some of the emotional sting out of death. So, talk to them about it. Make it seem like a journey we are keen to go on, talk about the folk we can't wait to meet again, say how excited we will be to see Jesus—after living the life He's called us to live on this earth. Allow for some temporary sorrow but assure them it will be worth it; convince them it will be much more fun than being a ghost!

Oh, and one more thing. When you are telling them all about where you plan to go, make sure they know how to follow you there!

When the perishable has been clothed with the
imperishable, and the mortal with immortality,
then the saying that is written will come true:
"Death has been swallowed up in victory."
1 CORINTHIANS 15:54 NIV

- Talk about family members who have passed over, and how wonderful it will be to see them again.

- Raise the subject in good times so it doesn't always have to be associated with grieving.

31. Think, "From Now On. . ."

You can find inspiration in the most unlikely of places! In the action romp *Cowboys and Aliens* Daniel Craig plays a man who has lost his memory and is trying to come to terms with who he is. A dying pastor tells him, "The Lord don't care who you were, Son, only who you are."

One of the most wonderful things in a faith filled with wonders is that, while we live, we always have the chance to start over, to be better, to be forgiven and grow closer to the Lord.

You messed up? Say sorry to God and start again. He will always accept a sincere apology, always give another chance. Such is the extent of His love.

So don't let your tomorrow be dictated by your yesterday. Focus on today and who you are. The Lord wants the best you can be right now.

Daniel Craig's character had to lose his memory to hear those words, but we can hear the equivalent each time we turn to God with a repentant heart. Yesterday, with all its faults, is gone. Be better today.

I have blotted out, as a thick cloud, thy transgressions,
and, as a cloud, thy sins: return unto me;
for I have redeemed thee.
ISAIAH 44:22 KJV

- Take a moment on your knees. Sincerely ask forgiveness. Rise renewed.

- Extend the courtesy of a fresh start to others, in God's name.

Authentic FAITH

32. Walk in Love

Do you remember your first love, when you walked on fluffy clouds and spent a lot of time hugging yourself?

Have you ever watched a little child walk along beside his mom in a shopping mall? So long as Mom has the child's hand, everything is fine. Take Mom out of the picture, and the child is instantly in a nightmare of fear and confusion.

Intellectually, we know that God loves us more than that first boyfriend or girlfriend. We might talk about how He is closer to us than a comforting hand. But do we show any of that in our daily walk through the world?

Take the love you read about in the Bible out for a walk, stroll with your lover/beloved, listen for His whispers, know that He is head over heels about you and will never cheat on you.

Walk in so much love that others will want to come along.

And walk in love, as Christ also hath loved us,
and hath given himself for us an offering and
a sacrifice to God for a sweetsmelling savour.
EPHESIANS 5:2 KJV

- According to the movies, if you "Whistle a Happy Tune," it will make you braver. Try keeping a catchy praise song near your lips to remind yourself how loved you are.

- Be God's love for others who are lost or worried.

33. Let Go of Bitterness

So a guy walks into a crowded room. He's carrying a sack and there is a snarling, ugly animal in it. The guy's friendly and chats to everyone, but the other folk in the room are fascinated by the sack. He generally ignores it, but just having it there produces a strained quality to his conversation.

Are you waiting for a punch line? There isn't one. That's just what it's like when we carry a grudge. Other folk generally don't want to know about it, and even though we think we have it under control and it's not doing any damage, we don't, and it is!

God is all about relationships. Things that get in the way have to be got out of the way. The grudge (usually made up of our pride and self-importance) has to be set free to run back to its unpleasant master. Then we have to go about our Father's work and love each other. He isn't joking about that!

Looking diligently lest any man fail of the grace of God;
lest any root of bitterness springing up trouble you,
and thereby many be defiled.
HEBREWS 12:15 KJV

- Sometimes people won't apologize and sometimes they can't. You can alter the situation for the better by moving past the need to receive an apology.

- Leave the past in the past. Then ask God how He wants today to be.

34. Recognize the Enemy's Work

Now, you might think of the devil as a guy with horns and goat legs, or you might think of him as some nebulous malevolent force, but there is no doubt that something works against the good.

If we want to be on the side of good, then we need to be aware not only of what pleases the Lord, but of what prevents us from doing those things.

If something comes between you and a friend, makes you turn away from a stranger, or plants hurt and resentment in your heart, you need to recognize that "something" for what it really is: the enemy of good.

Then we need to go further, because these things will disguise themselves as part of us, so we will hold onto them. Having recognized "him," we need to tell him he is not us and is not welcome. Then we patch up the damage he did and move on—as children of the good!

*I have given you authority to trample on snakes
and scorpions and to overcome all the power
of the enemy; nothing will harm you.*
LUKE 10:19 NIV

- Nothing will beat you as easily as something you prefer not to think about. Watch out for his work.

- Having recognized his work, you will soon see he is subtle but unimaginative. Learn to anticipate, then enjoy sidestepping him.

35. Praise in Deed

So, why do we praise God? Because He deserves it!

But consider this. Who would you rather spend time with, people who are thankful and appreciative or people who are always complaining?

Imagine if you were to set out each day with the intention of praising the Lord with your deeds, actively looking for things to do that would make Jesus smile.

Now, that wouldn't be easy. It would require some mental and emotional discipline. You might have to overcome shyness and embarrassment. In carrying out those kindnesses you might have to hone your sensitivity, work on your tolerance. It would certainly increase your understanding of, and probably your love for, humankind.

Would you be a better or worse person for all the above?

Sure, we praise God because He deserves it. But I wonder if He had that little side-benefit—that it makes us better people—in mind all along.

In the same way, let your good deeds shine out for all to see,
so that everyone will praise your heavenly Father.
MATTHEW 5:16 NLT

- Begin the day asking God what you ought to do. End the day asking Him what He thought you could have improved on.

- Repeat the above, daily.

36. Do Little Things with Love

Perhaps you are a mom who spends her days doing things no one even notices, let alone appreciates. Perhaps you spend your days in a boring, repetitive work environment where no one seems to care what you do until something goes wrong.

It is sometimes difficult to give your best, to be your best, if it seems as if no one notices.

Now imagine how God's "day" is spent. With immense power He keeps the universe, and all those galaxies, solar systems, and planets spinning in their prescribed orbits. But He also teaches the bird to make a nest, tells the apple when to fall, grows a flower on a mountainside, provides earthworms to keep our soil fertile, gently heals the cut on a little boy's knee, and so on.

No matter how much He is praised, He is still the most underappreciated "person" around. But He does all those little unnoticed things because they are just as important as the big things in His grand scheme.

So, if you are tempted to do less than your best with some task you think no one will notice, remember, God notices. And He appreciates all your efforts.

Do the little things the way He does—in love!

*He that is faithful with little things is faithful with
big things also. He that is not honest with little
things is not honest with big things.*
LUKE 16:10 NLV

- Find something to thank God for in everything
  you do, from the littlest thing on up.

- Remember, those small unnoticed acts are the
  foundations you build your life on. Do them
  well and thank God that you can.

37. Give Credit Where Credit Is Due

I do a lot of good. But I will reword that!

There's a joke where scientists challenge God to a life-creating contest. "No problem," says God. He reaches down, picks up some dirt, and fashions a man. The scientists nudge each other and smile. "We can do that, too," says one scientist as he fires up his equipment and reaches for the dirt. "Not so fast," says God. "First. . . make your own dirt!"

When I do good, all I do is reallocate the time, the money, the food, whatever, that God has provided me with.

We can do nothing without Him, so we ought not to get too pleased with ourselves when we do good. But don't let that take all the fun out of it! Thank God for the good that has been done, thank Him for the provision that allowed it, and especially thank Him for allowing you the privilege of being His feet, His hands, and His smile!

You will find it is actually more wonderful than taking the credit for yourself!

"Yes, I am the vine; you are the branches.
Those who remain in me, and I in them, will produce
much fruit. For apart from me you can do nothing."
JOHN 15:5 NLT

- Praise God for everything you do. His was the gift of breath and body that allowed you to do it.

- When you help someone out with something, mention His name. Let them know who is really helping.

38. Practice Patience

Impatience is a very difficult thing to do good with. It conjures up images of anger, harsh words, pushing on ahead. . . . Sometimes we manage to hold those aspects in check and still achieve some positive things—but usually at the expense of the feelings of the person who made us impatient in the first place.

Don't get me wrong, impatience can be good, but you charge through a minefield when you give in to it. You might get all the way across that minefield without doing any damage, but the odds are against it.

So breathe deeply. Take the long view. We are on a journey to heaven. What could possibly compare to that or should be allowed to distract you from it?

You will need to have patience on your way to that destination, because when you arrive there is up to no one but God. Until then, don't let impatience over trivial stuff turn you into the person you wouldn't want to present at the Pearly Gates.

Say not thou, I will recompense evil; but wait
on the LORD, and he shall save thee.
PROVERBS 20:22 KJV

- When you feel yourself getting impatient, ask yourself if you truly believe God has things under control. If you do, you probably won't feel the need to rush Him.

- Take the time you would normally spend being agitated and spend it talking with God about something completely different.

39. Keep Good Company

This is a difficult one! If you only keep the company of other believers, then how do you spread the Word? On the other hand, if you only keep company with unbelievers, you risk being taken along their path!

As always, the answer is to look to Jesus. He kept company with all sorts—but followed none of them. He didn't hesitate to take the message to the Jews, the Samaritans, the tax collectors, the priests. And when He walked on, He took those who heard with Him.

Likewise, don't shy away from any particular group. If God puts them in your way, then there is probably at least one person there who will benefit from what you have to say. Sit a while and talk, but make sure that when you start walking again you are still heading in the right direction. You may take some with you—or they might start their walks later because of you.

Keeping good company also means being part of a fellowship of faith-minded friends and drawing strength from one another but, first and foremost, it means keeping company with Jesus. After that, "good company" means anyone—from whichever social group—who wants to hear about Him or who would like to meet Him.

Thou hast a few names even in Sardis which have
not defiled their garments; and they shall walk
with me in white: for they are worthy.
REVELATION 3:4 KJV

- Refuse company with no one but, remember,
  you have your own journey to make.

- Be prepared to welcome new traveling
  companions and to say some farewells. Pray for
  both groups.

40. Ask, "Will It Do Me Good?"

Golden retrievers are beautiful dogs, and Stella is no exception. But she does have a penchant for rolling around in smelly stuff. The smellier the better as far as she is concerned!

Of course, as a dog, she has no conception of how beautiful her golden coat is, so she sees no need to keep it clean.

Humans are prone to similar behavior. We put "junk" inside us and "inappropriate" clothing around us. Physically and emotionally, we sometimes wallow in some seriously malodorous stuff and convince ourselves it makes us happy.

But we have an advantage over Stella. We know what we are. We just need to remember it more often and treat ourselves appropriately. We might not be "golden," but we are something better: We are the chosen children of the Creator of the universe. That should be enough to encourage us to shine!

Ye are all the children of light, and the children of the day: we are not of the night, nor of darkness.
1 THESSALONIANS 5:5 KJV

- I heard a mom tell her child, "If you couldn't explain it to your grandmother, don't do it." Think of grandparents as God's representatives!

- Replace "It won't do me any harm" in your thinking with "Will it do me good?"

41. Get Involved in Renewal

Some folks prefer things to stay the same, while others are drawn to new things.

Unsurprisingly, God does both! His core principles are eternal, but He keeps them forever fresh and young by constant renewal.

As proof of this, we have the seasons and each new day. We have the way generation follows generation and the way burned grassland will be green again the next year.

Hold tight to your core values (as long as they are also God's) but don't stagnate and don't let them grow stale. Find new ways to apply them. Get involved in the next generation, help a new project get on its feet, restore something old. You will find ample opportunity to use, or even install, those core values in the new venture. In doing so, you will give it a firmer foundation and give those values (and the person who holds them) a new lease on life.

God is about renewal and rebirth. Join Him in it as often as you can.

*He saved us, not because of righteous things we had done,
but because of his mercy. He saved us through the washing
of rebirth and renewal by the Holy Spirit.*

TITUS 3:5 NIV

- Remember all earthly things pass, and that's a
  good thing. Don't mourn the old when you can
  help with the new.

- See each renewal in your life as a practice run
  for the great renewal in heaven.

42. Encourage Others to Do Good Works

Okay, sometimes the only way to get a thing done is to do it yourself. That's fine if it's short-term and if you're in a hurry. But if it is something you hope will last, then you are either going to have to be immortal, or you are going to need others.

The kind of good work God wants done isn't the "here today, gone tomorrow," kind. It's the kind that would transform the world if only enough people took part.

Strange as it might seem, a lot of people don't know what it is God expects of them. That's why those of us who do know owe it to the future, and to the Lord, to tell people what needs doing, to teach them how it is done, and show them the wonderful rewards that come from such works.

Because we are not immortal—just yet—we ought to aim for more than just doing those good works; we ought to raise a generation who will surpass us in them.

And let us consider one another to provoke
unto love and to good works.
HEBREWS 10:24 KJV

- Be patient with those who aren't as capable as you. You weren't always as capable as you are now.

- Share stories of positive outcomes to encourage others to try. But give the credit to God!

43. Find the Greatest Story in Other Stories

What makes a good story? You know, the ones that tug at your heart and live on in your memory. There might be an unlikely hero, insurmountable odds, a sacrifice made in love, betrayal, a hint of something greater at work, a happy ending (even if it does involve a lot of tears).

Christ's life, death, and resurrection isn't called "The Greatest Story Ever Told" for nothing. His story is our story; it speaks to the very essence of our being; and the great stories we read, see on TV, or watch at the movies will almost certainly have elements of it in them. That's why they mean so much to us. You might even see aspects of it played out in other people's lives.

Once you start looking for them, you will see bits of the Greatest Story everywhere.

And there are also many other things which Jesus did, the which, if they should be written every one, I suppose that even the world itself could not contain the books that should be written. Amen.

JOHN 21:25 KJV

- Every time a movie or TV program touches your heart, look out for the modern equivalent of biblical characters.

- Involve friends and family. Say, "Wasn't he as hotheaded but good-hearted as Peter?" or, "He's the Judas in this version," or, "Does that kind of loving sacrifice remind you of anything?"

44. Store Up Treasure in Heaven

We all know we can't take earthly treasure with us when we move on from this life, but we still tend to pay it more attention than the kind we can pile up in heaven.

When my daughter was very little, she had a toy pirate ship. It had a little brown and gold treasure chest that she would regularly bury in my rose garden and promptly forget about, until she accidentally dug it up again, days or weeks later. She was delighted and amazed every time!

The burying meant that she didn't play with it day-to-day, but the joy it brought her that way was so much greater.

The works we do in this world in God's name are like that. They won't benefit our everyday life, and they might cost us something. But we will rediscover them in heaven and get to see all the good they did. And our joy at rediscovering that treasure will know no bounds!

> *But lay up for yourselves treasures in heaven,*
> *where neither moth nor rust doth corrupt,*
> *and where thieves do not break through nor steal.*
> MATTHEW 6:20 KJV

- Don't rest on past glories. Rise each day determined to serve Him anew.

- Look on acquiring heavenly treasure as a game with the ultimate happy ending, if you like. But only play it in a spirit of service.

45. Enjoy Surprise Siblings

Once the stores have closed, this particular mall stays open all night. Access at one end is by escalators or elevator. The lady with the walker was repeatedly pressing the call-button for the elevator to no effect.

I walked over to tell her they were always switched off in the evenings, when the doors slid open and she stepped in. Surprised, I looked around and saw the security camera. On an impulse I raised a thumb. The public address system crackled and a disembodied voice said, "You're welcome!"

As surprising as it may seem, we are constantly surrounded by friends we haven't met yet and some we might never meet, but that won't stop them from helping. Despite a lot of noises to the contrary, we *are* a family under God, and we will often be surrounded by brothers and sisters without knowing it.

A spiritual gift is given to each of us
so we can help each other.
1 CORINTHIANS 12:7 NLT

- The next time you stumble, look to see how many people reach out to help.

- Be a surprise brother or sister to someone else.

46. Don't Respond Negatively to Hurts

How do you respond when someone hurts you? I'm guessing, negatively.

The next time someone hurts you, try putting your reaction on hold. You know the old idea of counting to ten before you respond. A faith-filled version of that is to recite ten words before responding. Our. Father. Who. Art. In. Heaven. Hallowed. Be. Thy. Name.

Hurts, no matter who inflicts them, don't come from God. They come from an altogether less pleasant source. And, if we add a negative response, we are only pouring gas on flame, reinforcing the bad.

On the other hand, doesn't it seem weak not to respond aggressively? How feeble is it to respond to hate with love? So "feeble" that strong men and powerful nations often can't do it.

So the next time someone inflicts a hurt, don't fuel the fire, don't give the devil what he wants. Take the higher, harder way—after counting to ten, of course.

He that is slow to anger is better than the mighty;
and he that ruleth his spirit than he that taketh a city.
PROVERBS 16:32 KJV

- Understand that people inflict hurts from a position of fear or weakness, even if they don't understand it.

- Nothing people can say or do to you affects your standing with God. Respond as one who is secure in that love.

47. Be Led by the Spirit

I offered him lunch, though I was too busy—and discovered he hadn't eaten for three days. He had prayed that morning for the first time in a long time. I walked past the elderly lady and turned around for no reason—only to discover she had just asked God for someone to help carry her groceries.

There is a level of communication beyond radio signals, beyond anything telecom companies can offer, beyond the Internet. I was picking up on that.

Be prepared to listen with an open mind and a willing heart. Go along with the little voice that doesn't make sense (but still seems good), until you see God's purpose in it.

It's like a foreign transmitter on an old-fashioned radio dial. The more you tune into it, the easier it becomes to find. The difference being that, in this instance, it isn't a foreign transmitter after all—it's a message from home!

Trust in the LORD with all thine heart; and lean not unto thine own understanding. In all thy ways acknowledge him, and he shall direct thy paths.
PROVERBS 3:5–6 KJV

- Cultivate peace of mind. The signal will come through clearer without all that interference.

- Never be surprised if what the Spirit seems to be saying doesn't make sense. It will in God's time.

Section 2

AT CHURCH

48. Sing!

You know the old stories of genies in bottles? The traveler who found the bottle always had to remove the cork to let the magic out.

To a greater or lesser degree we tend to live buttoned-down, bottled-up lives. We have a face for our families, a face for the boss, perhaps an uglier face for the guy who cuts us off in traffic. But when does the real person we are get to come out?

I'm going to suggest—when we sing!

Of course, it helps to have others singing around us, so we can't hear those pitch problems, so we don't have to worry if we sing the occasional wrong word.

Find a song that speaks to your soul, lift your head, pull the cork and let the magic out—the magic that is the real you, singing joyfully to the real God.

> *"Shout aloud and sing for joy, people of Zion,*
> *for great is the Holy One of Israel among you."*
> ISAIAH 12:6 NIV

- Don't concern yourself with whether or not others can hear you. Sing so the Lord can hear you!

- More important than the correct words or the correct tune is the correct attitude. Sing joy. Sing praise.

49. Worship. . .Together

It's a unifying thing!

Wherever you get a sizable group of people, there will be divisions and differences. There might be people in the congregation you don't know or aren't sure about. Until you worship together at the foot of the cross!

If there are still people who don't talk after that, then they must have missed something. In a group of committed believers, the people who weren't sure about each other up until that point now know all they need to about each other: that they all love God.

It's a good theory. And it's up to us to make that theory a reality. When we meet in the love of the Lord, we need to include everyone in that love. We become stronger for the experience, the congregation moves closer together, and the body of Christ becomes a healthier, stronger one.

So worship together in love. You and your brothers and sisters in the Lord will be better for it.

What then shall we say, brothers and sisters?
When you come together, each of you has a hymn,
or a word of instruction, a revelation, a tongue or
an interpretation. Everything must be done
so that the church may be built up.
1 CORINTHIANS 14:26 NIV

- There is usually a time of fellowship in churches. Use it to get to know more of God's children.

- The love of the Lord is common ground to stand on. Everything else, personalitywise, is negotiable.

50. Actually Go to Church

Church used to be the place everyone went to on Sunday. In some communities, people would be expected to turn out to a four-hour service in the morning and a similar one in the evening.

Recently the church has suffered from an image problem. It's no longer a cool thing to do or an interesting place to go.

The institution perseveres, and it tries to do its best in a changing world. But if you're not going to church because you don't like its image, you are missing the point. You are the church. Go along and change the image. Maintain the core values, but revitalize them, apply them to your life; give them new life. Show the world that the church—both the people and the institution—are still relevant, still vital!

And you can't do that unless you go.

Keep watch over yourselves and all the flock of which the Holy Spirit has made you overseers. Be shepherds of the church of God, which he bought with his own blood.
ACTS 20:28 NIV

- Be an actively involved in the church.

- When you are tempted not to go, ask yourself who is doing the tempting.

51. Support Your Church

Our treasurer often jokes, "I'd like to publish the church expenses every week—but I don't want to scare people away!"

Unless you meet in a field, your church will require upkeep. Your relationship with that idea will say a lot about whether you are at the right church or not.

If you go along every week, hoping not to be noticed but hoping to hear a good word, then, dare I suggest, you aren't really committed to that place or those people. If your church is a place you feel you belong, if the congregation feels like family, then that is the church for you, and you will probably be happy to help keep it going.

As to how you do that—well, it depends on your circumstance. You might tithe, you might offer what you can when you can, or you might offer service in some way. But you will be part of the church, with a vested interest in keeping it going. The one thing you won't be is scared away.

In the same way, the Lord ordered that those
who preach the Good News should be supported
by those who benefit from it.
1 CORINTHIANS 9:14 NLT

- Support your church and expect to be supported by it in times of need.

- If you don't know how your church is financed or what it does with those finances, ask.

52. Fellowship

Fellowship is generally portrayed as a wonderful thing. But it can be frustrating!

The idea is that we learn from each other, encourage each other, and are stronger as a group than we are alone. It often works that way and can be a beautiful thing. But sometimes it can be a trial—and that's when more is asked of us.

That's when we may have to accept that maybe it isn't the other person who is weird—perhaps we aren't perfect! We may have to humble ourselves for the greater good of the congregation. And God does some of his best work in our humility! Without the barriers of pride and independence, the congregation is stronger and the fellowship deeper.

So whether fellowship is easier or more difficult, persevere. One way or the other, it will be worth it!

With all lowliness and meekness, with longsuffering, forbearing one another in love.
EPHESIANS 4:2 KJV

- You often have to get to know people before you get to know if you can help them. Socialize with your fellow churchgoers.

- Remember, everyone there will be fighting their own battles. Reinforce them with your love.

Section 3

IN THE WORLD

53. Enjoy Music

When George Frideric Handel wrote the *Messiah,* which went on to become, arguably, the most famous choral piece in the world, ever, he had tears of joy rolling down his cheeks. Later, he would say he felt as if he had been elevated to the court of heaven.

Music does that.

There is no earthly reason for music. But the desire to make music and to appreciate it is a basic one for mankind. Why?

Could it be, perhaps, because it fills our minds, cutting us off from the worries of the world, and opens up a highway to the heavens?

If we want to take a break from the world, we often use music as a beautiful barrier between it and us. The world wouldn't supply us with a means of stepping away from it, so music must come from elsewhere.

Accept it as a gift from God; then do what Handel did and meet Him in it.

> *It is good to praise the LORD and make music to your name, O Most High.*
> PSALM 92:1 NIV

- King David thought music an excellent way to worship God. Perhaps we should try it, too.

Whatever the genre, choose life-affirming music.

54. Go Outside

You know those characters you see on TV wearing aluminum foil hats? The idea is that they believe aliens are sending signals to their brains, making them do crazy stuff, and the aluminum foil blocks those signals (as if that, in itself, doesn't qualify as crazy stuff!)

Now, God can talk to us anywhere, but we tend to fill our homes and our workplaces with *our* stuff, with *our* expectations and experiences, with family and work colleagues, with deadlines and soccer runs, and so on. All that can be a more effective barrier than any aluminum hat.

Stepping outdoors, hopefully somewhere away from traffic and buildings, stepping into just a little of the great wide open, clears the channels of communication. The signal that comes through there might still make you do "crazy" stuff, like being more loving, feeling more loved, and walking about in awe of God's creation.

You can certainly talk to Him in your home, but don't forget to pay Him a visit out there in His, too.

And the earth brought forth grass,
and herb yielding seed after his kind,
and the tree yielding fruit, whose seed was in itself,
after his kind: and God saw that it was good.
GENESIS 1:12 KJV

- Visiting the same place at different times will
  show you just a little of Creation's endless
  variety.

- With all that natural awe, you are going to
  need someone to share it with. Take a friend!

55. "Bathe in the Woods"

If you're lucky enough to live near a wooded area, then why not go for a bath in it?

In the East there is a tradition of Shinrin-yoku, or "wood air bathing." It is thought that the trees "breathe" out natural compounds that impart a feeling of well-being. Some even claim they give health benefits.

Of course, proving such a notion must be all but impossible. But, if you've enjoyed a leisurely walk in the woods, you might give the idea some credence.

These compounds seem to have no use—except to make us humans feel better. Kind of a free gift from God. Enjoy!

Then shall the trees of the wood sing out at the presence of the LORD, because he cometh to judge the earth.
1 CHRONICLES 16:33 KJV

- Enjoy the tranquility of the woods, but watch out for lions and tigers and bears, oh my!

- Take the time to thank God for the blessings we often don't see—or understand.

56. Consider the Water

Water. So, what of it?

It lies around in puddles; it flushes our sewers. We mix it with detergent, shampoo, and soap then watch it disappear down the drain.

Animals walk in it, animals drink it, animals. . .well, you know. . . .

But that stuff has been around forever! In the first moments of creation, God was hovering over the waters. That's how old it is! And, it's still the same water. No new H_2O has been added. But no matter how badly we treat it, it runs through a God-provided system and is renewed, is as fresh and life-giving as it ever was.

If you want an easy example of how God redeems, scoop a handful of water from a stream, think what it's been through, and look how pure it can still be.

> *And the earth was without form, and void; and darkness was upon the face of the deep. And the Spirit of God moved upon the face of the waters.*
> GENESIS 1:2 KJV

- Tumbling over rocks and waterfalls oxygenates and cleans water. We might look at turbulent times in our lives as similarly cleansing.

- Thank God for the life-giving properties of a simple glass of water.

57. Appreciate Art and Beauty

Have you ever just stopped and stared at a sunset or a spectacular view? I'm sure you have.

Have you ever tried to create art, whether it be a nicely framed photograph, a full-blown painting, or just drawing in the dust with a stick? Again, I'm sure you have.

Any visit to a museum or art gallery will show you that the desire to create art and the appreciation of beauty have been part of human civilization for longer than there has been any kind of civilization.

If this world was all about survival, especially in earlier, harsher times, beauty and art would have been worse than useless. They would have been positive distractions in a "survival of the fittest" type of world.

But still we do it, still we yearn for it. Because in our dreams and in our souls we know there is something more beautiful than this world to be aspired to, and, until we get there, we will soothe our souls a little by trying to recreate a little of heaven's beauty here on earth.

For the entrance to the courtyard, make a curtain that
is 30 feet long. Make it from finely woven linen,
and decorate it with beautiful embroidery in blue,
purple, and scarlet thread. Support it with four posts,
each securely set in its own base.
EXODUS 27:16 NLT

- The temples and altars of the Lord have always been decorated in beauty. Make your art a similar tribute.

- Use your art, or your appreciation of it, as a way of drawing closer to the source of beauty.

58. Marvel at Big Things

Stand in front of something vast, be it the desert, the ocean, the mountain. Then realize that this vastness is only a part of the world, and the world is only a part of the solar system, and our solar system is a tiny part of the universe.

How small do you feel now?

But, like no other creature, you have the ability to comprehend all this. You have the ability to rise above mere survival. You can love, you can cry, and you can laugh.

So, what makes you so different? Why isn't this insignificant little creature simply getting on with getting on? Because the Creator of that vastness gave you something special—a direct link to Him.

We are small, but we are not insignificant. We are the reason for the universe. Our smallness simply reflects how much God has given us!

> *What is man, that thou art mindful of him?*
> *and the son of man, that thou visitest him?*
> PSALM 8:4 KJV

- Stand under a starry sky on a clear night and imagine the power of the Creator.

- Visit the redwoods or the ocean and appreciate the life that flows through them.

59. Get Away from the Noise

Nature isn't always quiet. Streams gurgle, winds howl, animals and insects make a fascinating variety of noises. But grass grows silently; trees grow silently; animals, despite their noises, do their growing quietly. Even in our modern, bustling world, God seems most often to do His work silently. (Excited and amazed humans might make a noise about it, but He tends to move and work very, very quietly.)

If at all possible, we owe it to ourselves, every once in a while, to get away from the hustle and the noise, to somewhere we can put bare feet on grass, where we can't hear the traffic in the distance, where we can lie back, feel the fertility of the soil, and be caressed by the breeze on our cheeks.

Then we can just lie there in silence and grow along with the rest of His creation.

The Lord is in his holy temple;
let all the earth be silent before him.
HABAKKUK 2:20 NIV

- Without the distractions of noise, listen to your breath and the blood in your veins—works of God we hardly ever notice.

- Without the distractions of noise, become more aware of your need to belong.

60. Find God in the Animals

Saint Francis of Assisi preached to the birds in the trees and the animals in the fields. Was he crazy?

No, he just saw God in all creation. The birds, the rabbits and the sheep were, as far as he was concerned, brothers and sisters in God's greater family.

Now, some people might argue with that, but not pet owners, I imagine. Anyone who has ever looked into the eyes of a contented pet will surely see some of God's love there, a love untainted by human concerns. That unvarnished affection is what makes contact with animals such an effective therapy in some children's wards and senior citizen's centers.

The world and the animals may have been given for mankind to "steward," or look after, but that doesn't mean God can't love us through them or that we can't love Him back through them.

Now the Lord God had formed out of the ground all the wild animals and all the birds in the sky. He brought them to the man to see what he would name them; and whatever the man called each living creature, that was its name.

GENESIS 2:19 NIV

- When you hear tales of animals rescuing humans, ask yourself where that love comes from.

- Ruling over (or looking after) the animals was the first duty God gave man. Show Him we still take it seriously by giving love to an animal in need.

61. Stop to Smell (and Consider) the Flowers

He and I argue about faith all the time. But I found him in his garden one morning staring at a carnation. The frilly, compressed leaves were bursting out of their green-leafed bud like so many layers of a cancan dancer's petticoats. I asked what he was thinking, and he was big enough to admit he was puzzling over how such a thing could happen by accident. He readily admitted science couldn't hope to replicate the process.

We take things like flowers and trees and grass for granted because they are everywhere and always have been, but they are amazingly complex organisms in an even more complex ecosystem, any part of which would be enough to take our breath away if we just looked closely enough.

They speak of the glorious splendor of your majesty—
and I will meditate on your wonderful works.
PSALM 145:5 NIV

- Spend time with growing plants and wonder how they do what they do and when they do it.

- Ask yourself why flowers are beautiful. It surely can't be for the benefit of the bees!

Section 4

_____

WITH THE BIBLE

62. Read the Bible

Centuries back, only the church had Bibles. People had to attend services to hear the Word of God read aloud. Then we reach a point where it seemed as if every home had one. The Bible became like part of the furniture. Perhaps that was when people stopped reading it.

Isn't that often the case? If a thing is scarce, we will travel miles to see it, but, if a thing is easily available. . . yeah. . .we'll get around to it sometime. And the Bible sits there, as important as ever, but neglected.

Perhaps the Bible needs better PR. Maybe we need to remember that this book has massively outsold every other book that ever existed and has probably been banned in more countries than any other piece of writing. Why? Because of the power imbued in it by its author!

Let's not wait until someone tries to take it away before we value it. Let's sit down, get comfortable, and find out what it's all about.

Jesus answered and said unto them, Ye do err,
not knowing the scriptures, nor the power of God.
MATTHEW 22:29 KJV

- Take up a Bible reading program or read it as part of a group.

- Don't settle for having read it once. Read the Bible throughout your life.

63. Expect Difficult Questions

I once told a friend I had started reading the Bible from the beginning—and stopped at Joshua! All that warfare and bloodshed! No thanks! That was as far as I wanted to go.

He asked me to imagine a path through a forest. "You get so far and you find a big rock on the path. You push it, but it won't move. You can't dig under it or climb over it, so you turn and go home. Then you hear that beyond the rock the woods end and the path goes into a valley that is surely paradise on earth."

I agreed I would be pretty upset at missing out on that.

"All you had to do was walk around the rock."

Don't be put off by the difficult bits in the Bible, and, likewise, don't be disheartened by the tricky questions others ask you about it. God is supposed to be beyond understanding. You aren't supposed to understand all His works. But you will—when you get to the "valley."

God's voice thunders in marvelous ways;
he does great things beyond our understanding.
JOB 37:5 NIV

- Just as there are different ways of learning, there are different ways of knowing. Don't be flustered by people demanding explanations on their terms. Be content with wonder and mystery.

- If the Bible were man made, it wouldn't be so hard to understand. Persevere, knowing that the "difficult" bits are often what ensures its authenticity.

64. *Memorize Verses*

I'm not against tattoos, but I can't imagine many designs or words that would mean the same to me when I was eighty as they did when I was eighteen. It would be too late to have regrets after the tattoo was done.

My biggest problem would be finding something that I wanted to live my whole life by.

When it comes to whole-life wisdom and beauty, the Bible is definitely the place to look.

When I find a verse that really impacts me, a verse I want to keep near me, I read it and reread it. I repeat it. I close the book and try to recite it. Repeat and repeat, like the hundreds of little pinpricks that build up a tattoo. Except I'm not printing the verse on my skin, I'm taking it deeper than that, making it a part of my memory, a part of my heart, part of the person I am.

I don't ever regret that.

"This is the covenant I will make with the people of Israel after that time," declares the LORD. "I will put my law in their minds and write it on their hearts. I will be their God, and they will be my people."
JEREMIAH 31:33 NIV

- Learn verses not to teach others but to remind yourself.

- As you memorize the verses, allow yourself to be filled with the beautiful words of the Lord.

65. Read the Bible Aloud

Do you ever skip bits when you're reading? I know I do. Lengthy description, dense explanations, my eyes slide quite easily over those bits to get to the drama.

Or it might be that we've read the book before (hopefully, several times in the case of the Bible), and we slip into reading what we think is there rather than what is actually there.

With reading out loud there are no shortcuts. You kind of have to give every word its due. Better than that—you start intoning, adding emphasis and pauses. You almost put yourself in the position of the person writing. And in the case of scripture, those are some interesting shoes to be standing in.

Want to find yourself closer to the people who wrote the Bible? Read it out loud. Maybe just not on the bus or train!

But what does it say? "The word is near you;
it is in your mouth and in your heart," that is,
the message concerning faith that we proclaim.
ROMANS 10:8 NIV

- If you can read the Bible aloud to someone else, then two people benefit.

- Read it slowly. Read it with feeling.

66. Join a Small Group

Back when I was a teenager, I knew it all. I didn't know Jesus, but I was fairly convinced I knew everything that mattered. And I couldn't imagine anything more boring than a small-group Bible study!

Of course, the older you get, the more you realize how little you know.

One of the more amazing things about the Bible is that it speaks differently to each of us. When we read through a piece as a group, it is often surprising what other people take from it.

I'm old enough now to know how little I know. And the Bible constantly reminds me that I am only beginning to understand its layers upon layers of complexity and usefulness.

Small-group Bible studies help with that. I get to understand my Bible, the Bible of my neighbor, the Bible of the guy sitting across from me, the Bible of his daughter, the Bible of the guy I don't know all that well yet. . . .

It's the same book, but with so much to learn from it that it often takes a group to really get started!

Then opened he their understanding,
that they might understand the scriptures.
LUKE 24:45 KJV

- Make sure everyone gets the chance to share
  what God has put in their hearts.

- Give every view due consideration and allow
  for the possibility of your own understanding
  being expanded. God may be talking to you
  through your small group.

67. Meditate on Scripture

Imagine you could combine the narrative of a novel with the depth of a philosophical work. What would you have then? Something like the Bible?

Yes and no. Yes, because the Bible is a fascinating story that we can get more out of every time we read it. No, because no combination of books or literary styles produced by men will ever result in a book that actually talks to us.

God needs to be involved for that to happen. We ought never to stop reading the Bible, because God will never be finished talking to us. The words don't change, but the same verse will say different things to us at different times. So we need to take our time, savor the words, turn them over in our minds, and say, "Lord, tell me the same old story—how I need to hear it today!"

I reach out for your commands, which I love,
that I may meditate on your decrees.
PSALM 119:48 NIV

- Make Bible reading a part of your relaxation. Relaxed, you will be more open to God's thoughts.

- Find a convenient way to take the Bible with you so you might read it in different situations.

68. Encourage Others with Scripture

Have you ever heard anyone complain that life doesn't come with a book of instructions? Well, of course, it does. If you find a situation that didn't exist in biblical times, then you will usually discover it's only a variation on a theme already covered.

Those answers can often be set in some dense language or archaic situations. Set yourself the task of finding those "instructions" and translating then them into everyday language. Then, when a friend needs a word of wisdom you can casually say, "There was a situation like that in the book of. . . ."

You might encourage others to turn to the Bible in the future. Or, at the very least, you will be giving them advice that was written specifically for them—by the manufacturer of their life, in the instruction manual He made to go with it!

> *The eunuch asked Philip, "Tell me, please,*
> *who is the prophet talking about, himself or someone else?"*
> *Then Philip began with that very passage of Scripture*
> *and told him the good news about Jesus.*
> ACTS 8:34–35 NIV

- Take a situation from your life and search for the nearest biblical equivalent.

- Remember, societies and lifestyles have changed since then, but human nature remains the same.

69. Make the Bible a Part of Your Family Life

Once upon a time it seemed as if every home had a family Bible.

It's a tradition worth reviving, either for our own generation or the next. Find a Bible you can dedicate to your family life, one that will go with you from home to home. Read to your children and grandchildren from it. Let them know they can read from it themselves any time they like. Keep a family tree inside the front cover and photos of a generation gone by behind the back cover. Put Easter cards the children made between the pages telling about the resurrection and special Christmas cards by the nativity. Write notes in the margins and encourage the children to write their questions there also.

Pass it on when you prepare to meet the Author.

And that from a child thou hast known the holy scriptures, which are able to make thee wise unto salvation through faith which is in Christ Jesus.
2 TIMOTHY 3:15 KJV

- Choose a sturdy, well-made Bible, one suitable for generations of children's interest.

- Treat it with respect, but always make it accessible. The scratches and tears will simply become part of its family history.

70. Relate Bible Stories to Your Life

The books of the Bible weren't always written at the times of the stories they record, but the world wouldn't have changed so much between the enacting and the retelling.

The world is hugely different now!

But the biblical lessons usually have more to do with the people involved than the situations they found themselves in. And people haven't changed.

It's still entirely possible to be caught up in jealousy, as Saul was. Families might still turn on each other, as Joseph's brothers did. Parts of the world are no less hostile to our Christian message than where Daniel met the local lions!

Find your modern equivalent of the stories, decide what the lesson was, and apply it—in real life! You might find the God-inspired results are worth writing a book about!

For everything that was written in the past was written to teach us, so that through the endurance taught in the Scriptures and the encouragement they provide we might have hope.
ROMANS 15:4 NIV

- If your life was a Bible story, which character would you be? And what does that suggest to you?

- How would different biblical characters live your life? What might you learn from them?

Section 5

IN LIGHT OF THE
COMMANDMENTS

71. Love Thy Neighbor

Loving your neighbor can be more difficult than loving your enemy. There is generally a distance between your enemy and yourself. Your neighbor lives where you live!

If you don't do it properly, or if your neighbor rejects your attempts, there is no hiding place.

But just because it's difficult doesn't mean you shouldn't try. In fact you are specifically instructed to do it. If it works, then you and your neighbor will be stronger together. In fact the strength will be out of all proportion to the effort it took, precisely because you are neighbors.

Remember God is building a great big family, and once you move beyond your own immediate relatives, the next stop is. . .your neighbors!

The second is this: 'Love your neighbor as yourself.'
There is no commandment greater than these.
MARK 12:31 NIV

- You might have to wait to be invited into their lives, but you can invite them into yours.

- Don't just love the neighbor who is your kind of guy or gal. It's equally important to love the folks who aren't.

72. Reach Out to Your Enemy

It's an oft-quoted example that, when Abraham Lincoln was urged to destroy his enemies, he said he would destroy them utterly—by making them his friends. And that is what God wants.

Imagine you had lots of kids. How many of them would you like to see left out of group activities? How glad would you be to see some of them attacking or ignoring the others?

We are all God's children—and He wants us to get on.

Of course you can't *make* people be friends with you. You can't *make* your enemies become your friends. What you can do is find a way to span the gap between you and keep it open even if they rebuff you, so that, when they finally see how serious you are, they can walk onto the bridge you built and meet you in the middle.

Imagine how you would smile if you saw a child of yours do something like that!

> "You have heard that it was said, 'Love your neighbor and hate your enemy.' But I tell you, love your enemies and pray for those who persecute you."
> MATTHEW 5:43–44 NIV

- Be a peacemaker. You will be blessed.

- If you can't entice your enemy in, then at least refuse to close the door.

73. Care for Widows and Orphans

Religion is a multifaceted thing these days. Often the divisions and denominations are caused by long-established customs or prioritizing one aspect of the faith over another.

It's nothing new. In the times of the apostles there were divisions and debates as to what the true faith consisted of. Jesus summed it all up beautifully: Love God and each other; love each other as I loved you.

James narrowed it down: Keep yourself pure and look after the widows and orphans. Widows and orphans were simply the most vulnerable people in society at that time—and may still be.

Show your love of God where God's children need it most. It may mean a visit and a chat or something more substantial. But, whatever your denomination, make sure you practice true religion.

Religion that God our Father accepts as pure and faultless is this: to look after orphans and widows in their distress and to keep oneself from being polluted by the world.
JAMES 1:27 NIV

- Look for the vulnerable. They won't be immediately obvious. People disguise vulnerability in many ways.

- Don't let the commitment or the seeming magnitude of the help put you off. If you take the step, God will provide the resources.

74. Care for the Sick

Hospitals have a very faith-based history. Monasteries and chivalric orders would set themselves up as "hospitalers" or people providing hospitality.

The Bible is keen on promoting hospitality. Jesus rebuked a man for his lack of the hospitality due to a guest. We are told to show hospitality to strangers because they may be messengers of God.

That's all well and good, but caring for the sick does something for us as well. It teaches us selflessness, patience, humility, self-sacrifice—all things that bring us a little closer to the pure souls we ought to be.

In showing hospitality to strangers, we may entertain angels. In caring for the sick we may, without meaning to, raise ourselves just a little bit higher than angels.

And he sent them to preach the kingdom of God,
and to heal the sick.
LUKE 9:2 KJV

- Try to earn your home a reputation as a place of hospitality.

- Don't just visit: take God's love to the sick.

75. Care for the Prisoners

Care for prisoners? Those guys are in jail for a reason!

So what is that reason? Oh, yes. They are sinners! Well, any casual reading of the Gospels will tell you how interested God is in them!

Not everyone will be in a position to help prisoners, but we can be pen pals, send cards, offer a fresh start to someone who has served time.

Prisoners are often doubly incarcerated. They are locked away from the world, and their habits, upbringings, or addictions often lock them away from the love that might lead them to the Lord. Evil often has them in a cage no one can see. Love is the key to that cage.

Will you offer it, for God's sake?

Naked, and ye clothed me: I was sick, and ye visited me:
I was in prison, and ye came unto me.
MATTHEW 25:36 KJV

- Help in practical—but constructive—ways, encouraging progress.

- Forget their sins and focus on their redemption.

76. Care for the Homeless

A member of my family was sleeping on the street. Searching for him, I found myself in a soup kitchen in the midst of a group of aggressive homeless guys. I think they thought I was there to take some of their food. Twenty minutes later they were hugging me and saying they would pray for me.

Why? Because I was doing for my brother what they hoped someone would do for them: looking to bring him home. (Which I did!)

People become homeless in this word for various reasons, but there is one home where we will all be gathered in love. The invitation has been made. Some just need to be assured that the invitation really was even for them, too!

Suppose a brother or a sister is without clothes
and daily food. If one of you says to them, "Go in peace;
keep warm and well fed," but does nothing about
their physical needs, what good is it?
JAMES 2:15–16 NIV

- Notice, James doesn't say "homeless person" or "hobo," he says "brother" and "sister."

- Get involved in an aid program. If God's love isn't at the center of it—put it there!

77. Forgive

There was a castle near where I live. Only the foundations remain. It stood, defying all enemies, for hundreds of years. When that kind of conflict fell out of fashion, it went into decline. Finally, it was too expensive to keep going. Wind, fire, and rain did their work.

Locals used stones from the walls to build homes, many of which are still standing today.

Some people say that forgiveness is weak. The implication being that not forgiving is somehow strong. It depends on your definition of strength.

Would you rather build walls of stony defense, walls of unforgiveness, keeping people out like the old castle? Or would you rather use your strength to break down walls and build homes for families?

Don't forgive and stand in solid defiance of all comers, or forgive and let life flourish around you. You get to choose.

And be ye kind one to another, tenderhearted, forgiving one another, even as God for Christ's sake hath forgiven you.
EPHESIANS 4:32 KJV

- Forgiveness needn't be a big deal. Often it involves no more than a conscious decision to walk on past the dispute.

- The other person might not accept your forgiveness, but you and God will know it was given.

78. Repent

Repent! That word's come to be seen as the equivalent of "Woe is me!" or "The end is nigh!"

The biblical writers didn't mean for us to fall on our faces weeping. They meant, "Think again! Look again at your life! Turn your mind and your life toward God!"

Why was the call even necessary? Because we get so tangled up in the things of the world that we lose sight of God. It is as true now as it was then.

So set yourself a regular reminder; perhaps in your diary, perhaps before church every Sunday morning, perhaps in some alone time at the end of each day, and repent. Say, "Hey, God. How am I doing? Have I strayed a little? I'm sorry. Bring me back beside You, Lord."

Make the necessary adjustments as you go and travel onward, content that "woe" is not you and, if the end is nigh, it will only be the end of your earthly distractions and the continuation of your heavenward journey.

I say unto you, that likewise joy shall be in heaven over one sinner that repenteth, more than over ninety and nine just persons, which need no repentance.
LUKE 15:7 KJV

- See repentance less as a punishment for failure and more as an opportunity for growth.

- Not sure what needs repenting of? Anything that distances you from God.

79. Participate in the Sacraments

Jesus didn't tell us to fix a fish symbol to our trunk. He didn't tell us to wear a nice, tasteful cross on a chain, but He did tell us one way to remember Him.

As important a part of church life as the communion ceremony often is, the original meal didn't take place in a church or any other consecrated place (unless we accept that the upper room was consecrated by Jesus' presence).

In the end the place where we partake of the bread and the wine is less important than the fact that we are doing something in remembrance of Him. And wherever we remember Him, that place will be consecrated by His presence.

While they were eating, Jesus took bread, and when he had given thanks, he broke it and gave it to his disciples, saying, "Take and eat; this is my body."
MATTHEW 26:26 NIV

- The ceremony might be ornate or basic, but you take the love to it and the remembrance from it.

- Take your worldly desires to the altar; then, in communion with Jesus, swap them for His.

80. Count Your Blessings

We are told to count our blessings all the time—but rarely do. Why? Perhaps it is because we are so blessed that the idea of counting them all is quite a daunting one. Sometimes we have to narrow the field a little.

I was on a train, surrounded by about twenty squealing, laughing, drinking, young women who were heading toward a raucous bachelorette weekend. They weren't due to get off the train for another three hours!

I was tempted to be annoyed. Then I wondered if my response was more down to me that the situation. So, I tried counting my blessings.

I found I was in the company of women setting out to celebrate a marriage—a good thing, surely. Their love and support of the bride-to-be was obvious and would hopefully continue.

My attitude changed completely, aided not a little by my happiest realization—that I had music on my phone and earphones to plug into it.

Suddenly, it was all a blessing!

Wherever you go and whatever you do, you will be blessed.
DEUTERONOMY 28:6 NLT

- It's too easy to default to disapproval. Put the effort into actually looking for blessings, and you will be rewarded.

- Be prepared for counting your blessings to become a lifetime activity!

81. Feed the Hungry

Wow, feeding the hungry is a big ask! There are just so many people in need! What can any one individual do?

Well, we can look to the examples of Jesus and those around Him. He didn't search out the hungry. They came to Him and were hungry, so He fed them. But He didn't create the food He fed the five thousand with out of thin air—although He could have. Instead he took a humble gift, freely offered, and worked wonders with it!

To be able to help global organizations feed hundreds of thousands is undoubtedly a good thing. But most of us will find "the hungry," one person or one family at a time, in front of us at some point in our daily lives. We probably won't be in a position to change their lives, but we can do what the little boy with his loaves and fish did. We can make a free and loving offering from what we have; we can do it in Jesus' name. And we can trust that He will make something wonderful out of it.

"But we have only five loaves of bread and two fish!"
they answered. "Bring them here," he said.
MATTHEW 14:17–18 NLT

- Offer to have lunch with someone living on the streets.
- Remember the hungry that aren't so obvious, like moms on a restricted budget.

82. Guard Your Tongue/
Speak Life

What has been the most destructive weapon over all of human history? The sword? The automatic rifle? The H-bomb? A very good case could be made for. . .the tongue!

How may invisible cuts have been inflicted by harsh words? How many lives have been twisted by things said by people who were, themselves, victims of verbal cruelty?

But that same tongue also has the power to speak life, to sing praise, to give comfort, to lift people's spirits, to share words of love!

We tend to use it casually, and our default option can often be careless, rude, or thoughtless. Given all the damage that can be caused or all the good that can be done, it's usually a wise thing to think before you speak. Think love. . .and then speak life!

> *The words of the reckless pierce like swords,*
> *but the tongue of the wise brings healing.*
> PROVERBS 12:18 NIV

- Often remind yourself of the good you can do with a few kind words.

- Take time to search for good things to say. Then enjoy the life-affirming effect they have.

83. Keep the Sabbath

Every time someone makes a rule, someone else, in their enthusiasm, will take it too far.

Over the centuries, some place or another, practically everything except going to church has been illegal on the Sabbath. Court cases have been fought to maintain its purity.

So, just what is the Sabbath? It's a day set aside for men and women to remember their God. Whether they remember Him in restful contemplation or devote the day to activities that please him really isn't important. What is important is that, in this increasingly busy world, they spend time with the Lord.

Rules and court cases aren't what will keep the sabbath pure. The love and contemplation each of us put into it will take care of that!

Six days shall work be done: but the seventh day is the sabbath of rest, an holy convocation; ye shall do no work therein: it is the sabbath of the LORD in all your dwellings.
LEVITICUS 23:3 KJV

- The Sabbath is a great time to have a family day. A meal, a prayer, a loving family. God would surely smile!

- Or simply take time off from the activities of the rest of the week; talk with God, count your blessings, that kind of life-affirming stuff.

84. Have No Other Gods/ Don't Worship "Graven Images"

What does it mean to worship a graven image? It goes something like this—you take something man made, prostrate yourself in front of it, and make it the focus of your life.

Ask yourself, is there anything like that in my life? The television, perhaps? Your laptop? Your favorite beer? That closet full of clothes?

If it comes between you and your partner, if it takes up time you could spend with the kids, if it keeps you from going to church—walk away from it.

Make God and His works your focus. Then, if you have any time left over, you can spend some of it with your "idol." But you might find that, after spending enough time doing "God stuff," you really won't want to do anything else!

*Ye shall make you no idols nor graven image,
neither rear you up a standing image, neither shall
ye set up any image of stone in your land, to bow
down unto it: for I am the LORD your God.*
LEVITICUS 26:1 KJV

- Find the habit, interest, or activity you just "couldn't" give up; then, just for a while perhaps, and just to show your real priority, devote its time to God.

- You probably don't have false gods in your home or your workplace—but do you have reminders of God the Father?

85. Don't Kill

That's pretty self-explanatory. What else needs to be said?

Well, there are lots of different ways of killing. We might kill someone's self-respect with our words. We might kill someone's dream through our lack of support. We might be killing ourselves with our habits.

Basically, if we are bringing someone down in any way—including the most serious way, where we bring them down and they never get back up again—then God says don't!

Thou shalt give life, speak life, and encourage life. Thou shalt not kill.

> *Ye have heard that it was said of them of old time,*
> *Thou shalt not kill; and whosoever shall kill*
> *shall be in danger of the judgment.*
> MATTHEW 5:21 KJV

- You might be tempted to put someone down to score a point or because they hurt you. Think of it as possibly inflicting a mini-death. Choose life instead.

- Choose life for yourself as well, because we don't put people down without going part of the way with them.

86. Don't Lie or Steal

If you aren't in faith, you really won't care what the commandments say, although you might ask why you would want such negative stuff in your life.

For the person of faith, they are a whole different ball game. Yet some still lie, some still steal.

What are we thinking? Of course, the answer is—we aren't thinking! We aren't thinking through our faith or how great our God is. What lie can we tell that He doesn't already know the truth about? If we lie to save face in front of someone, imagine how embarrassing it's going to be when He asks us why that person was more important to us than Him.

As for stealing, if we don't have something, God didn't mean us to have it. Is it really worth the hold we give the enemy over us just to get it?

God knows and will provide. Hold fast to these truths the next time temptation starts enticing you.

Neither shalt thou steal. Neither shalt thou bear
false witness against thy neighbor.
DEUTERONOMY 5:19–20 KJV

- Imagine lying in front of someone who loves you, someone who sees the fear and weakness that lead to the lie. Embarrassing? Foolish? It's what we do *every* time we lie.

- If God didn't provide something, we're better without it!

87. Don't Misuse the Name of the Lord

Much as we might sometimes wish it when we hear the language some people use, God is not going to smite anyone for taking his name in vain.

A certain three-word phrase beginning with the letters O, M and G has become everyday speech for some people who don't even believe in God. Dumb? Yup!

So, what do we do about it? Smite them ourselves? Not very loving. Take them to task? Probably pointless!

Maybe we ought to show them how the name of the Lord ought to be used. Perhaps we can claim it back if we speak it often enough, lovingly enough, in awe, in worship. . .in public!

Let's make it a name that's a challenge to the people who misuse it. Who knows? Then they might, eventually, come to love it!

Let them praise the name of the LORD:
for his name alone is excellent;
his glory is above the earth and heaven.
PSALM 148:13 KJV

- God's name is often used in frustration and anger. Make it heard in love and wonder.

- Talking about God might become habitual, but never let it become thoughtless. Remember the power of His name.

88. *Don't Commit Adultery*

God is about relationship! And He is ever faithful. His people try his patience regularly—and have throughout history. Sometimes He steps back. But He never leaves.

God, through Jesus, is the Bridegroom, and we, as the church, are the Bride. That marriage will last for all eternity.

So, you see, He is about relationship for the long haul.

Ducking in and out of a marriage is just like the Israelites turning to false gods. They debased themselves, and they broke God's heart. But He always took them back.

Marriage isn't easy, but overcoming the problems and temptations only makes it stronger. God always loved His people beyond imagining, but for us mere mortals that kind of love is only acquired by hanging in there for the long haul—as He has.

But a man who commits adultery has no sense;
whoever does so destroys himself.
PROVERBS 6:32 NIV

- Life is short, so you have to get your happiness where you can, right? Wrong. Life is short, and real happiness awaits those who can get through it in style, with fidelity and faith.

- Not happy in your marriage? Then you partner probably isn't either. With God's help, add more love to the mix.

89. Honor Your Father and Mother

When my daughter became a mother, she was the most prepared she had ever been for anything. But that first week floored her.

Motherhood is one of those things that no one can fully explain to you. You have to experience it for yourself to even begin to understand it. Fatherhood is the same—in a different way!

When God says, "Honor your mother and father," He doesn't say why. You just have to take His word for it. If you aren't a parent, you won't understand. If you are a parent, then you probably already do honor those who showed you how it was done.

It's no surprise that God should include moms and dads in His list of priorities. He is, of course, the ultimate parent!

Honour thy father and thy mother: that thy days may be long upon the land which the LORD thy God giveth thee.
EXODUS 20:12 KJV

- Most of us will never be able to repay our parents for all they have done for us. It's like our relationship with God, on a smaller scale. You can't repay, so appreciate!

- Know that even if they wave your thanks away, you will have warmed their hearts!

90. Care for the Elderly

My grandmother had reached the point in her life where she needed a wheelchair to get out and about. I used to visit on nice days and take her out. She enjoyed the walks but was embarrassed at being pushed along.

"You shouldn't have to do this," she said.

"Well, fair's fair," I responded. "You did it for me."

"When did I do this for you?" she wanted to know.

"When I was a baby," I said with a grin. "Before I could walk."

"Ahhhhh." She settled back and enjoyed the rest of the journey.

After Adam and Eve fell, God made death so mankind would taste it and come to rely on Him all the more. But He also gave us generations so we might help each other in turn as we walk toward Him.

> *"Stand up in the presence of the aged, show respect for the elderly and revere your God. I am the LORD."*
> LEVITICUS 19:32 NIV

- God puts us, helpless, into the world and takes us, helpless, out of it. Those of us between those two events are the help He provides.

- The vulnerable occupy a special place in God's heart, as, I am sure, do those who help them.

91. Don't Covet

God gave this commandment to Moses and the Israelites some hundreds of years before Jesus walked on the earth. After Jesus' ascension, the apostles shared all their possessions. As a family they were stronger, as individuals they were more free.

They knew that we don't really "possess" anything. God provides things for us and takes them away again, all in His own time.

Besides, possessions can often be metaphorically piled up to separate us from each other and from God. Whatever it is your neighbor has that you desire may actually be bars in the prison cell he has built around him. Don't borrow his bars to build a cell of your own. Be free!

Thou shalt not covet thy neighbour's house,
thou shalt not covet thy neighbour's wife,
nor his manservant, nor his maidservant, nor his ox,
nor his ass, nor any thing that is thy neighbour's.
EXODUS 20:17 KJV

- The more we have the less we appreciate. Learn to be content with little—and appreciate it all the more!

- Your neighbor, who owns all that cool stuff, probably covets someone else's possessions. Refuse to go down that road.

92. Don't Judge

Despite it being a wintery day, my neighbor—a woman in her twenties—was still dressed in loose summer clothing. The sides of her head were shaved. The hair that was left was dyed purple. She had tattoos across her chest.

I asked what her plans for the day were, placing a mental bet they would involve day-time TV and kids running riot.

She told me she was working on the final paper for her accountancy degree!

I had judged—and been a fool to do so.

Sometimes we judge (negatively) and get it right, without having any idea of the hurt or abuse that went into creating the situation. So we get to be right and wrong at the same time.

Judging is a loaded game. The devil operates the table, and we leave ourselves open to *being* judged simply by walking up and placing our bet.

Judge not, and ye shall not be judged:
condemn not, and ye shall not be condemned:
forgive, and ye shall be forgiven.
LUKE 6:37 KJV

- We will probably always have opinions, but we should always be willing to change them.

- The best way to judge someone is to judge them a child of God, worthy of loving.

Section 6

IN PRAYER

93. Pray at Meal Times

There is no appetizer like appreciation when it comes to making sure you enjoy your main course. If this life is an appetizer for the main course that is heaven, then we should fill it with as much appreciation as possible.

Okay, it might take a little courage to hold hands and offer up thanks to God in a restaurant with other people around. But if you do it with style, if you do it with enough love and a smile on your face, if appreciation is radiating out from you, you never know. . . .

Someone at another table might just be tempted to tell the waitress, "I'd like some what they have."

They devoted themselves to the apostles' teaching and to fellowship, to the breaking of bread and to prayer.
ACTS 2:42 NIV

- Unless you grow your own food, there will have been many people involved in bringing the meal to your table. Take the opportunity to pray for them.

- Involve all the family, asking them each to contribute a thank-you for some blessing.

-

94. Pray on Your Knees

Kneel to pray. Why? It's embarrassing. It's old-fashioned. I don't have the time. I can pray hailing a cab.

Yeah. We can use all those excuses, and they are difficult to argue against. You literally can pray anywhere at any time. But I realized something about kneeling. It doesn't make the prayer better. It makes the pray-er better.

You see, we are complex beings. We can be nice, we can be pains, we can be kind, we can be arrogant. Well. . . you know.

But when the better side of me kneels down, humbling myself before God, it takes the not-so-wonderful side down with it.

Kneel, not because God deserves it (although He does) but because in humbling the part of you the devil works with, you will rise a better Christian.

> *O come, let us worship and bow down:*
> *let us kneel before the LORD our maker.*
> **PSALM 95:6 KJV**

- Kneeling to pray can be a private affair, but if you feel the need to kneel in public, do! People might stare—but God will be glorified.

- You needn't kneel if it causes discomfort. Kneeling in your heart is just as acceptable.

95. Talk Honestly with God

How many people are we completely honest with? Honestly.

We might flatter friends to make them feel better. We might "lie by omission," not saying what we really feel, because keeping the peace is more important to us. We might tell our boss that report is practically completed then work on it all through lunch.

Sometimes being less than honest seems just what it takes to keep the wheels turning smoothly.

But God knows everything about everything. You can't deceive Him, and He won't deceive you. There is no other relationship like it.

Go to Him in absolute, vulnerable, honesty. You might find yourself being completely honest with yourself in the process, and only good can come of that!

If we had forgotten the name of our God or spread out our hands to a foreign god, would not God have discovered it, since he knows the secrets of the heart?
PSALM 44:20–21 NIV

- Sometimes the truth shows us in a bad light. God knows that side of us and loves us anyway.

- The truth doesn't only set you free; in God's hands it also heals. Offer it to Him so He may give you freedom and healing in return.

96. Be Always in Prayer

Pray constantly. It's a big task, isn't it? Except, it isn't. It's a wonderful thing.

I'm sure lots of folk over the ages have devoted themselves to lives of seclusion and rounds of repeated, prescribed prayer. That might be what this means. But I prefer to think it means making prayer an everyday part of your life.

I heard recently of a wife praying the supermarket would have a half-price chicken while her husband prayed he would find a parking space. Not wishing. Specifically asking God.

When I cross a busy road, I ask God to see me safely home. (I don't specify which home.)

Praying constantly isn't about chanting or reciting Latin. It's about having a dialogue with God about even the smallest aspects of the most ordinary day and knowing He's interested, knowing He's listening, and knowing he's responding.

My friends got their half-price chicken and their parking space.

But we will give ourselves continually to prayer,
and to the ministry of the word.
ACTS 6:4 KJV

- God is God, but I'm sure He doesn't mind if
  you talk to Him like a friend.

- Talking to God in constant prayer is
  affirmation, if it's needed, that He is always
  beside you.

97. Pray as a Family

Children derive a lot of security from being part of a loving family. They like to know their parents can take care of them. How much more secure will they feel if we raise them in prayer, teaching them that their family is vast beyond imagining and that there is someone loving them whose power dwarfs even Mom's and Dad's?

Families do, of course, go through stages, and children become teenagers and often rebel against authority figures. But if, all through their childhood, they have seen Dad and Mom bow before a higher authority, who are they going to rebel against?

For a wife and a mom there can be few things more satisfying than bringing her family, all together, before the Lord in prayer. The phrase "well done, good and faithful servant" comes to mind.

And for the father, the husband, who will normally lead the prayer, it is a reminder that he's not the boss, he's simply in a position of responsibility—and that should encourage him to pray even more.

*When it was time to leave, we left and continued
on our way. All of them, including wives and children,
accompanied us out of the city, and there on
the beach we knelt to pray.*
ACTS 21:5 NIV

- Use discretion so family prayer time doesn't become something people feel they have to do but, rather, it is something they want to do.

- Daddy or Mommy might lead the prayer, but allow everyone to have their say in their own way.

98. Pray for Your Pastor

The apostle Paul used to say it was his job to get to the people and open his mouth. What followed was God's work.

Your pastor might wish it was that easy! Sermons don't prepare themselves, week after week, year after year. And it's not like writing a report for school. The things he says will touch people's hearts—and that's a big responsibility.

When you don't see him in the pulpit, he'll probably be dealing with situations you would be glad not to have laid at your door (as well as good stuff like baptisms and weddings.)

If he's any kind of human being (and he probably is) he won't just shuck all that hurt and drama off when he hits the couch. He almost certainly bears a load you don't know about.

For the love of God and your pastor, spare the fellow a prayer if you can.

*So Christ himself gave the apostles, the prophets,
the evangelists, the pastors and teachers, to equip
his people for works of service, so that the
body of Christ may be built up.*
EPHESIANS 4:11–12 NIV

- Pastors are the Christian equivalent of frontline troops. They are where the battle is fiercest. Support yours in prayer.

- If you can lighten your pastor's load in a practical way, then do so. But you will help him most by raising him in front of the Lord.

99. Make a Sacred-Time "Date Night"

Having children is a wonderful experience, but it can put quite a restriction on your romantic life. Smarter spouses explore the possibility of "date night," a specific time when, no matter what the expectations of the little ones (or the cost of babysitting) may be, they can spend time with each other.

All too often our relationship with God is full of distractions. We love Him, but. . .there is so much stuff that needs taken care of! Because God doesn't complain, we let time with Him slip down our list of priorities, and our relationship suffers. This is what couples who still have date nights are trying to avoid.

So set up a date night—or a sacred time—with God. Then do whatever it takes to keep those dates. Keep them sacred. Keep your relationship with the Lord at the top of your list of priorities.

But Jesus often withdrew to lonely places and prayed.
LUKE 5:16 NIV

- Make your sacred time and church the foundations of your relationship with God. Then build on them.

- Don't say, "I go to church, that should be enough." He doesn't just love you on Sundays.

100. Listen

I used to occasionally skip prayers because I had nothing to say.

Uh! What kind of conversation is that? Well, I'll tell you. I have a couple of acquaintances who love to talk to me. But they never ask how I am. If I take advantage of a gap in their conversation to insert something about myself, they wait patiently until I'm finished—then carry on from where they left off. As if I never spoke.

Ideally, it's best to listen to God all the time, but if you find yourself kneeling at the foot of the bed with nothing to say or sitting in the pew with a mind like a blank page—stay a while. Let God whisper into your silence or write an entry in your mental diary.

You will usually find the result of having nothing to say and listening instead gives you plenty to talk about.

The LORD came and stood there, calling as at the other times, "Samuel! Samuel!" Then Samuel said, "Speak, for your servant is listening."
1 SAMUEL 3:10 NIV

- Prayer is a two-way process. If we believe God knows everything, then we ought to listen as least as much as we talk.

- While you listen or wait to hear from Him, pray in silent love and submission.

101. Just Pray

Just pray.

We can talk about how to pray, when to pray, where to pray; none of that is as important as simply making sure you *do* pray.

Some people prefer a King James style when addressing the Lord; others prefer a more informal style. Some hesitate to ask Him for anything, assuming He already has it under control; others will take everything to Him in prayer. Someone I know restricts their prayers to thank-yous, while another friend sends short, sharp arrow prayers up throughout the day.

Don't be told which style suits you best, find that out for yourself. But do pray.

Why? Because, if ever you do seriously need a response to prayer, you will want to have practiced beforehand. But mostly because God loves you and not to keep in touch with someone who thinks so much of you would just be such a shame!

The LORD hath heard my supplication;
the LORD will receive my prayer.
PSALM 6:9 KJV

- Don't restrict yourself to any style or time. Pray when you need to or when you want to.

- You may not understand the response or its timing, but understand this—God loves you, and He will listen to you.

Faith Classics
from Barbour Publishing

Barbour's Faith Classics offer compelling,
updated text and an easy-reading typesetting,
all in a fresh new trim size. Introduce a new
generation to these books worth reading!

Confessions
by Saint
Augustine

The God of All
Comfort
by Hannah
Whitall Smith

Grace
Abounding
by John Bunyan

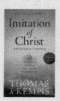

The Imitation
of Christ
by Thomas à
Kempis

In the
Twinkling of
an Eye
by Sydney
Watson

Quiet Talks
on Prayer
by S. D. Gordon

Each title: Paperback / 4.1875" x 7.5" / 192 pages

Available wherever Christian books are sold.